MEMORIES & MILESTONES

POEMS & PAINTINGS
BY
IRWIN E. THOMPSON

Published by Acanthus Publishing
a division of The Ictus Group, LLC
Unit 214, Union Wharf
Boston, MA 02109

Printed in the United States of America
10 9 8 7 6 5 4 3 2 1

Publisher's Cataloging-In-Publication Data
(Prepared by The Donohue Group, Inc.)

Thompson, Irwin E., 1937-
    Memories & milestones : poems & paintings / by Irwin E. Thompson.

      p. : col. ill. ; cm.

      Includes index.
      ISBN: 978-1-933631-63-9

1. Thompson, Irwin E., 1937- --Philosophy. 2. Artists--United States--Miscellanea. I. Title. II. Title: Memories and milestones

PS3620.H66 M46 2007
811/.54

Design: Erin Glennon

All Photography: Warren Patterson

Printing by:
Star Litho, Inc.
360 Libbey Industrial Parkway
Weymouth, MA 02189

With grateful thanks to Chérie, my wife and my mother, Sarah.

Thanks also to Barbara Helfgott Hyett, founder of PoemWorks, for her poetic guidance and to Warren Patterson for his imaging expertise.

contents

flood wrack ◆ 1

penumbrae ◆ 3

painting ◆ 5

negatives ◆ 7

bittersweet ◆ 9

origins ◆ 11

global warning ◆ 13

fractals ◆ 15

death and desire ◆ 17

barrier reef ◆ 19

shell games ◆ 21

rain forest ◆ 23

redwoods ◆ 25

the other world of trees ◆ 27

visiting Robert Frost ◆ 29

transition ◆ 31

remembrance ◆ 33

study in blue ◆ 35

divorce ◆ 37

correspondence ◆ 39

the return ◆ 41

sunrise at Suilven ◆ 43

after the party ◆ 45

check out time ◆ 47

plainsong ◆ 49

the burden of the y ◆ 51

via dolorosa ◆ 53

flood wrack

breaking swirls   drain
the weight
  of existence

boats and bodies
sweat   burning sex   and skin
primeval   i am

present on every beach
  washed
incessantly   ashore

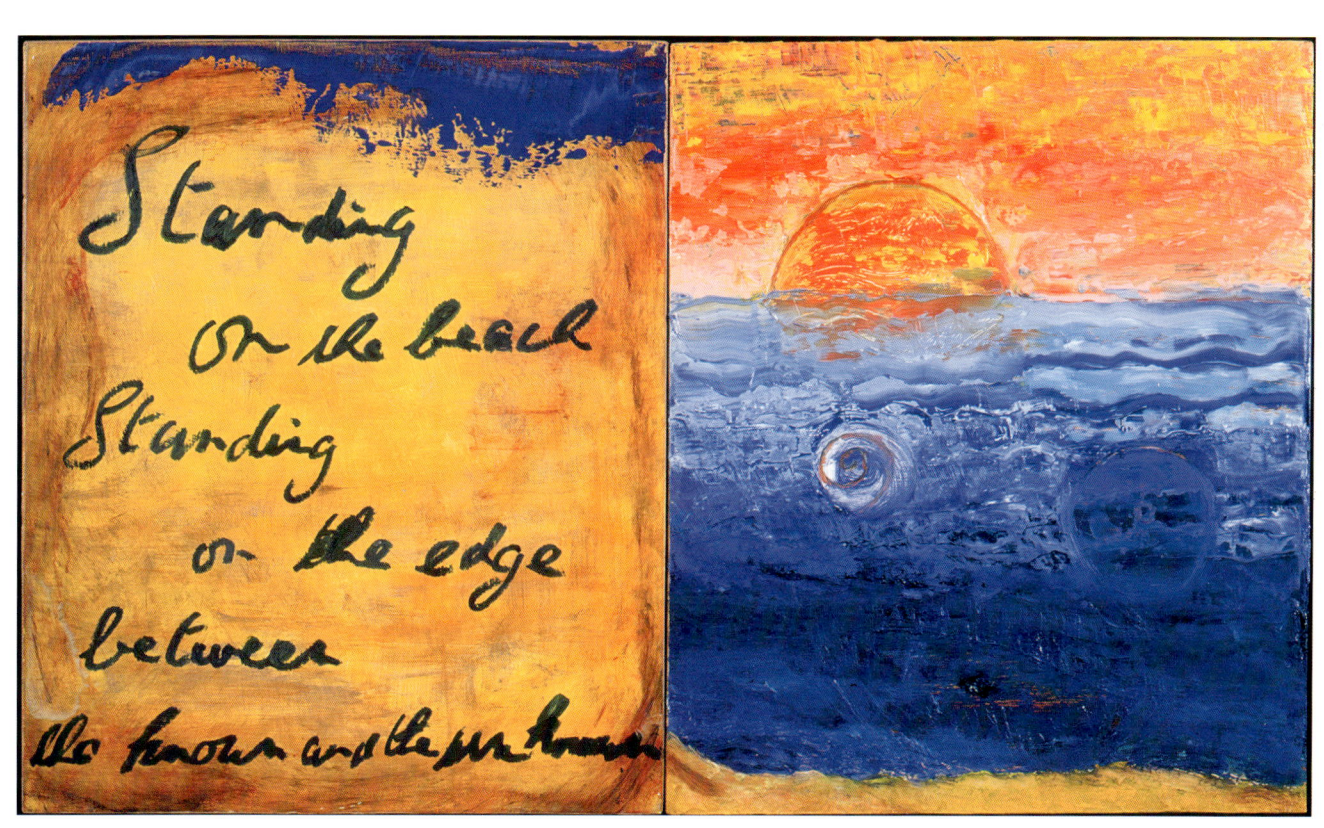

Standing
on the beach
Standing
on the edge
between
the known and the unknown

penumbrae

shadows
on the wall   moving
  blindly   perhaps
this is how
we appear

one
to the other   poised
on the surface
  of preoccupation

  darkly
adjacent   not truly
real
  never
to be touched

painting

a new nativity
   a fusion of genes and gels
smeared on naked

canvas   wounded by knife
soothed by brush
pigments   proliferate then

disappear
   and die
in their unnatural cycles

subjects of affection
   discarded without mercy
in the end   in a field

of cadmium red
the corpus callosum   bleeds
from my brain to my hand

negatives

clipped to fluorescence
x-rays of my hand
   a pennon
unable to grasp an eating fork
unable to grasp   a scalpel

 impaired
   the joint in my thumb
to be obliterated
   two small steel pins thereafter
   hold my life

bittersweet

the flowers of summer cope
with autumn   yellow trumpets die

on the vine   while the buds
of pink mandevilla shrink

  the canna lily droops   half-naked
as hosta withdraws

into itself
only bittersweet

  spurns   melancholy
glorious scarlet and orange everywhere

origins

the first blinding blaze
left
no weeping galaxies
  dark matter still
holding

nascent stars
collapsed
  dust across the universe
echoing light

superclusters
  fled
but the milky   way
stayed yellow
dwarf star   in its arms

and earth was filled
with   space
  until flesh

global warning

i've been thinking dinosaurs
fossil fabrications
  secrets
scattered everywhere   pangea
breaks apart

the polar cap and great glaciers
dwindle
  uncovering the loss
of realm

no blue Xerces   butterfly
 to flash
beneath the golden gate

fractals

the river flows
   constant
we are carried by that
current   understanding
as we may   or not

sudden   turbulent
   shift of wind
curls the fallen leaves
broken into spirals
   enigmatic whirls
like chaos itself

wild patterns disrupt
   irrational   rational
losing the way   finding
the way as Mandelbrot

 equated in his
   bifurcations
so it is with
   persons
in the dance

16

death and desire

incipient and
                    remote
as a mound
of bones   my mind
rises
to cognition

  a woman of the city
  casually sipping
the shimmering sunlight
from her glass
transparently dressed   as she was
in summer heat

i shiver now
  my gaze
was not   returned

barrier reef

i understand little
of extravagance

the blue light of the benthos
   phosphorescence
   odysseys of corals
in stygian caves
the community of sea dragons
   that want   to fly

shell games

the sacred chank
  stands carved
as a Chinese pagoda   whorls
and consecrated shapes

  floating
in a pelagic womb
of the world's warm seas
   the musical volute
   listens

the courtly cone
serves   a different muse
  its poison dagger
          strikes

rain forest

  twilight   thickets
     hide
in rot's regeneration
the journey   is obscured

parrots   squawk
in the tallest realm
and monkeys   howl
  at the setting sun

orchid   frangipani   ginger
  flower
the pernambuco tree
  its bows and strings
 silenced   in a new
   millennium

redwoods

how long they have breathed
in the fogs
ever living sequoia
assaulted   since the time
of gold   two thousand rings
   guillotined
without remorse
   the wind
   mourns
in the canopy
   of the unseen clerestory

the other world of trees

conceals the song of the mockingbird
  sap and blood
healthy and dying
beneath the weight
  of leaves
that wither   later
into truth

the marks of life
are borne
by cuts and bruises
green lichen   stains
disguised
as age

visiting robert frost

through green mountains
on little roads
　birches
stand sentinel
　fields
clothe themselves
in flower spikes

in the churchyard
i walk through sheets of rain
among epitaphs
and slabs
　caught
in summer lightning
brandishing his grave

this　a blessing
or is it　wrath

transition

as an unending   viking saga
another day of cold
and ice

  snowdrops rise
on the surface
and bluebells crowd their own
hearts   longing
  for yellow broom

gold linties   will wed
the fluttering sky
and the grief of winter
be overcome

remembrance

my mind slips
   sudden suffering   boys
in brown blazers
and George my best friend

   the others behind
underwater now
the fine fronds of his hair
   streaming
in the depths

i left him
diving like a dolphin
   how could he drown
in a blaze   of summer
no wind   no wave

study in blue

in full dress uniform
he stares seriously
   out
from his navy photo
   i see   myself
in the deep waves
of his hair

in another life
my lost uncle
   stays forever
vital   confident
in unknowing

in the periscope
   of time
he is leaving
the teen   age
of his life
to sail   into ice

divorce

25 years
had not prepared me
  we loved
in an attic nest
above the world
  equally enduring
so i thought

night
  after returning night
rue struggles
on my canvas
  leaving me   red eyed
in the inexplicable
conclusion

correspondence

the simple beauty of her
hand   the grace
of her lilting lines
   belie her words

the Scots don't speak
lightly of love.

stroke spreads through
her   eyes vacant
mouth disabled
     left arm relict
words useless

my mother   my correspondent
for sixty years
lies paralyzed
   aged   fallen
under
the wheels

the return

  we rumble
gentle in descent
as the quilt of land and loch
unfolds   from haze

first light
  void of gray and indigo
instinct   of pleasures
summers
into   purple night

mother   disregarding
death
you surrender into being

sunrise at Suilven

Suilven appears   slowly
out of the night

rock upon rock upon rock
    a soaring dominion   sandstone
crumbling battlements
chariots   grinding
  wind and ice

one thousand million
years   spilled
tumbling down forever
staining
the waters green

after the party

the last guest stumbles
into the numbing
dark   and i am clothed
   in the fabric
of the superficial

i sip my vintage port
   listen to the twelve string
fado   in that plaint

i undress
to welcome the ghosts
 of guests
 returning
we begin again

check out time

noon   outstays its welcome
the hourglass
of my life   once
almost empty   fills
   without consent
towards one last
recording image   then
   the void beyond

plainsong

chill   nocturnal
shadows leave

me alone with dawn
   and its distractions

certain monks   rise at four
to learn gratitude

   they flagellate themselves
in a ritual   of refuge

   chasten their bodies
before day begins

the burden of the y

we shelter our easels
   like ancient junipers
that grasp the canyon rim

painting   who we are and where
we are

   seeking the mutual grail
i   the solitary male
at the mercy of my gender

   isolated
among communicants

via dolorosa

i progress steadily   unsteadily
along the parabola

i have   discerned
mostly retrospectively

one thing leads   to another
  variation of chaos theory

maleness   as far as I was
unaware   became malignant

an assertion i succumbed to
  a statistic for survival

i celebrate   palingenesis
with a self-portrait

  a collage of my unconscious
for some sacrificial altar

index of paintings

after the party • 45 • diptych, oil on canvas

barrier reef • 19 • acrylic on canvas

bittersweet • 9 • oil on panel

the burden of the y • 51 • oil on canvas

check out time • 47 • oil on canvas

correspondence • 39 • oil, mixed media on masonite

death and desire • 17 • oil on canvas

divorce • 37 • oil on canvas

flood wrack • 1 • diptych, oil on canvas

fractals • 15 • oil, acrylic on canvas

global warning • 13 • oil on panel

negatives • 7 • oil on canvas

origins • 11 • oil on panel

the other world of trees • 27 • oil on panel

painting • 5 • oil on panel

penumbrae • 3 • diptych, oil, acrylic on canvas

plainsong • 49 • oil, mixed media on canvas

rain forest • 23 • acrylic on canvas

redwoods • 25 • oil on paper

remembrance • 33 • oil on canvas

the return • 41 • oil on canvas

shell games • 21 • oil on canvas

study in blue • 35 • acrylic on canvas

sunrise at Suilven • 43 • oil on canvas

transition • 31 • oil, mixed media on canvas

via dolorosa • 53 • oil, mixed media on canvas

visiting Robert Frost • 29 • acrylic on canvas